Servant of the LORD

BOOK ONE

Copyright © 2014-2015 Susehg Tsirch

Scriptures are quoted from:
The Holy Bible, King James 2000 Version
The Holy Bible, American King James Version

All rights reserved. In accordance with the U.S Copyright Act of 1976, scanning, uploading, electronic sharing, and distribution of any part of this book for commercial purposes without the permission of the Author, constitute unlawful piracy and theft of the Author's property. Thank you for your support of the Author's rights.

This book is based on the Author's real-life events; however, fictitious names are used for the entities that appear, to protect their identities. Any resemblance to real entities is entirely coincidental.

First Published by SkyOne Letters, 2014
Updated, January 07, 2015
Printed in the United States of America

ISBN 978-0-6923-2544-5

Servant of the LORD

BOOK ONE

From the Dunghill to the Palace: The Touching Life Story of a Shattered Vessel Remolded for a Divine Purpose

SUSEHG TSIRCH

SkyOne Letters

Emblem

GOD has united me with CHRIST - in His death and resurrection, and has thus obliterated my old life and given me an entirely new life. He has embraced me into His family and made me His son. He has made me His heir, and promised me an eternal inheritance with Him in Heaven. He sent the HOLY SPIRIT to dwell in me. I am therefore His temple.

THIS IS WHO I AM IN CHRIST!

Contents

Introduction: *How Do You Bless God?*

Dallas, Texas 15
The Treatment Center (I)

Life after the Treatment Center 23
A Poor Decision
Insanity at Its Finest
Soul-Searching
Detox Facility

The Treatment Center (II) 33

Oxford House 37

The Upper Room:
Father's Perfect Revelation 41

A Drink to Remember 49
The Intensive Care Unit

The Treatment Center (III) 59
Discovering Myself

The Home of Sobriety 65

The Voice 69
The Gift of Giving
Bible Lessons with Father

Great Miracles 77
The Cross
My Circumcision

Kingdom Assignment 81

My Trial: *Father by My Side* 85

Life after the Home of Sobriety 89
Undeniable Feelings
Twenty Twelve

My Consecration 97
A New Garment
A New Name

Introduction
How do you Bless God?

Blessing God was what I had thought about for quite some time, and wanted to do. Today, there is not a moment in my life that I do not thank Him. I make it a point to thank God on a daily basis - even for the simplest things. I wore the garment of *Ungratefulness* for so long in my previous life, but I am now a new creature. *Previous Life* refers to my life before my knowledge of God. Today, I am His cherished son and servant. I am chosen to be a witness of His faithfulness and tell a story that will change lives. I am a thirty-eight year old man, who has been to the dark places of the earth – places where human beings take the form of animals and live just like them. I was made to understand that each person had animal instincts. However, I did not realize the extent to which those instincts could overtake me. My eyes were wide open - just as they are today; but for so long, I was what you would consider, blind. I did not see what needed to be seen; hence, I continued to do much damage to myself. Darkness overshadowed me for a very long time. It rendered me incapable of loving myself, much less another human being. Who else but the Lord Himself can see through a man? (Jeremiah 17:10).

> **"The lamp of the body is the eye; therefore, when your eye is sound, your whole body also is full of light; but when your eye is evil, your body also is full of darkness."**
> **(Luke 11:34)**

From the age of seventeen up to thirty- two, not a day in my life was devoid of alcoholic beverage or controlled substance. I was at home one day wallowing in my filthy habits, when I ran into money issues. I had no money to get drugs. I offered my belt to a man who had what I needed.

He stared straight into my eye and said, "You would sell your soul if you could!" At that moment, I sat down on the couch wondering what a soul was, and how I could offer it. I had no soul, you see! I was a completely hopeless human being, living each day as though the next did not matter - wishing, hoping, and begging for either a drink of alcohol, or a hit on drugs. I was a thief, even though I was not a good one. I was also an excellent liar who could never see the truth to anything. Nonetheless, *Shame* and *Embarrassment* were normal emotions for me on a daily basis.

I am one of five children, but selfishly carried on like I was an only child. My parents would always say to me, "This household has so many problems. We beg of you; if you are not in any way contributing to a solution, do not bring a catastrophe." I never could separate myself from alcohol and drugs, even at times that I desperately wanted to quit having them in my system. It is amazing how the body craves the poison called

Alcohol and the mind seeks solace in it, as if life depends on it. *How could this be happening?* I wondered, so many times. My Heavenly Father always told me that a person who sought a thing that was not required to survive would seek it to their grave. If anyone ever thought of literally living two lives in one lifetime, it would only be possible by the power of God. God had existed even before the creation of the world. He is the same God today, who rules both Heaven and Earth from His Throne. From eternity to eternity, He is God (Psalm 90:2).

> Jesus said unto him, "You shall love the Lord your God with all your heart, and with all your soul, and with all your mind. This is the first and great commandment. And the second is like unto it, You shall love your neighbor as yourself."
> (Matthew 22:37-39)

I live a very spiritual life today. To me, being spiritual is living a lifestyle that is truly pleasing to the Almighty God. It is not about some religion that is practiced when and how we please; neither is it about identifying with a denomination or sect. Rather, it entails cultivating a personal relationship with God and loving Him with all our heart, soul, and mind. Likewise, we are to love our fellow human beings as much as we love ourselves and live peaceably with them. The fruit that the Holy Spirit produced in me encompasses these elements of righteous living. This lifestyle is how I have come to know to bless God.

CHAPTER 1

Dallas, Texas

It was July 2005. I had just turned thirty a few months back. My sisters and I were driving from Nederland, Texas to Dallas. I remember the year and month very well, but do not recall if my sisters were at Nederland to visit the family, or there on a mission to bring me down to Dallas. All three of my sisters were working and going to school in Dallas at the time. Moving anywhere beyond Nederland seemed like a very good idea to me. It was just what I needed. I was more than thrilled to be leaving the life that I lived at Nederland behind. Relocating from a small town to a big city was something I thought would do me some good – and it did at first. As we drove down to Dallas, I was thinking of just one thing: How things were going to turn around for me. I would seek employment, go back to school, and be a better person. I had always wanted to be a wonderful son to my parents, and a brother to my sisters. I wanted so much to be there for my brother, and craved to be a good husband to my wife. I longed to be the loving dad that my daughter would be so proud of, and a man with a sense of self-worth.

The Treatment Center (I)

On my third day in Dallas, I located a Treatment Center, downtown. I never knew such a place existed in my years residing in Texas - not even while I was on probation at Port Arthur. I had an assessment over the phone. The center subsequently approved me for treatment and contacted me three days later to check in. Words cannot describe how I felt. It was my very first time in treatment, and I was desperate for a change. I wanted to succeed in life. I wanted to prove to my family and friends that I could, and would change.

Those were my initial thoughts when I arrived at the Treatment Center, but I had no idea that I was lying to myself.

It was July 26, 2005. I checked into the center with my belongings. The center had three floors. The first floor accommodated counselors and technicians. The dining room (which was also our meeting room) had two large scrolls on the wall. If you were standing in the doorway, the two large scrolls would be on the wall to your right. I immediately thought of the movie, *Shawshank Redemption,* when I saw the scrolls, where instead of the poster covering a huge hole in the wall in the movie, the center had two large scrolls. There were also many pictures and paintings in the hallways, with inspiring words. Some mentioned something about God. I did not pay too much attention to the scriptures at the time.

My indifference to the scriptures on the pictures and paintings on the wall was not surprising. I come from a family that practiced Buddhism from generation to generation. We had statues in our home. My mom would offer fruits at the designated Buddhist altar we had at home, and light incense. She often instructed me to follow the same routine, but I did so merely out of compulsion, because of the respect and love I had for her. I had no idea what the Buddhist routine was about. It was also mandatory for me and my brother to attend a Vietnamese Buddhist Temple on Sundays. We knelt and prayed at the temple all the time, but I never understood a single word of the prayers we uttered; neither was I interested in praying. I do not know why it was difficult for me to cooperate with anyone at the temple, but I remember very well that meat was not served on Sundays. Sunday was a Vegetarian Day for them, and that was a big issue for me because I had to have a meat dish. Soon after, my brother and I found other pleasurable ways to spend our time at the temple. We looked forward to our regular visits there, as we would often dash to the gas station next door to play video games, right after our parents dropped us off. I grew up with many Catholic friends and drove past the community church in my area, but that was about it for me in terms of religious affiliations. I have come to realize today that, if you do not believe that a force greater than you are exists, you will begin to believe only in yourself.

As the days went by at the Treatment Center, I realized that I was extremely frustrated without a drink. Until then, I had thought that I was somewhat of a people-person, but found that I could not relate with other clients at the center. I just could not stand them. My attention was always on everyone, but myself. I was an angry man, and blatantly judgmental. I would sit in the dining room and literally wait for someone to offend me. Once, one of the other clients came to talk to me about turning my situation over to God. "Read this book and find God," he said to me. I got irritated at his kind gesture and almost tore his head off his neck. I responded in anger: "Who is this God that you speak of? Where is this God? Why are you speaking of a God, when you are here for treatment, yourself?" The center handed me a blue book. In it, the doctor stated that the only relief suggested for excessive alcohol intake and substance abuse was entire abstinence. *Entire abstinence*? I thought to myself. It was apparent that I had forgotten why I was at the center. I forgot all that I had planned to do to become a better person. I forgot that I needed to change for my loved ones and myself.

The thought of never having a drink again scared me. I knew and felt what was coming. I did not want what the center had to offer for recovery; neither was I ready to do what was needed to be done. I was honest with myself and knew that I needed an excuse to leave the Treatment Center. I thought of a very good plan to escape it all, and intentionally got into a fight with another client. I had reverted to my old self-destructive ways and did not even realize it. My action earned me an eviction notice from the center, there and then. In a matter of seconds, the brilliant plans I singlehandedly made to turn my life around all went down the drain.

CHAPTER 2

Life after the Treatment Center

Surprisingly, I stayed sober for eleven months after getting kicked out of the Treatment Center. Things were looking positive. I got a job at a restaurant in Plano, TX to wait tables, and lived with one of my sisters. Since I dropped out of high school in 1994 and subsequently dropped out of my first semester of college in 2003, I made a good choice to enroll in a community college to pursue a degree in Radiology. During my time there, I maintained a 3.6 GPA within three semesters. My plan was to finish two more semesters at the college and transfer to another one that was Downtown Dallas to get my degree. My sisters saw me doing so well and put funds together to get me a car. They drove a brand new 2005 two-door Honda Accord Coupe to my place of employment and handed me the keys.

A Poor Decision

It had been a year since I moved to Dallas. I had not been anywhere else but work and school. With that said, I was slowly getting to the point where I knew that a drink was near. I received a phone call from a friend informing me of a Bachelor's Party at an Adult Club. I paid my way into the club to meet with my friends for a night of fun. None of my friends knew the wonderful goals I had set for myself, my journey to success, and the progress I was making. The environment of the club and the long-time-no-see chats did some damage. In no time, I was doing my thing – drinking like a fish. The demon was back. I was consuming alcohol as though nothing spectacular had happened to me in the previous months.

I could not stop drinking for the next six months. I tried to juggle work, school, and drinking, but that did not work. Drinking for me at the time always led to drugs. Once that was established, the game was over for me. Needless to say that my seat in college was no longer occupied. I was now drinking recklessly and getting high on drugs in my apartment. An old girlfriend was in my life to rekindle our friendship while this was going on. She left after she witnessed my unproductive habits. This compounded my problems and made me drink the more. By November 2006, I realized that I had been drinking consistently since June. My attendance at work was almost perfect in the previous couple of months, but I was eventually fired. I found another job, and was fired, yet again.

Insanity at Its Finest

How does one define the word *Insanity*? I will give you my version. For me, sleep was no longer required. I also skipped showers for weeks. I was drinking and getting so high on drugs to the point where they overtook me. I would see things normal eyes would not see; hear things normal ears would not hear; and do things to myself that you can never imagine. Paranoia also set in. I began to fear that someone in the apartment was recording my activities and displaying them online. I would search all around the apartment for camera lenses. I believed that there were lenses in the electrical outlets in the apartment and began to seal them up with duct tape. The blinking lights on the smoke detectors were also camera lenses in my messed-up mind; so, I would get to the lights with a ladder and seal them all up. The TV set had a red light sensor that I thought was a camera lens. I took the TV apart and taped up the light. Then I dismantled the electrical appliances – the DVD player, toaster, videocassette recorder, and all other appliances, just to ascertain that nothing could be plugged into any of the electrical outlets. It was bad!

My apartment stank with dirty dishes. There were numerous ants crawling all over the dishes, and flies everywhere in the apartment. I would watch adult movies all day and skip daily showers, because I was afraid that someone would steal my drugs while I was in the bathroom. At a point, I began to speak aloud for no reason, and strongly believed that someone was in the apartment with me. I began to leave notes in my apartment, telling whoever was messing with me to leave so that I could have my drugs all to myself. I returned one day from getting drugs from a dealer, and looked at one of the notes that I had written. It was now apparent that something was terribly wrong with me, as I began to wonder who in the world could have left such a note (the note I singlehandedly wrote to my invisible guests) on my table. I dug through the notes of my college work looking for an answer to my puzzling question and asked aloud, "Who wrote this?" This madness continued for six weeks.

Soul-Searching

It was a very sad day in November 2006. I looked at the clock – it was 4am. I started to cry on my knees. I had been in this situation year after year. Times had changed, but I had not. I glanced at the TV; the words: *Don't You Start Crying Now,* were on it. I had lost grasp on reality. If there was a boundary between reality and lack of it, I had crossed it without knowledge. After a good cry, I looked at my drugs and told myself, "There is no reason to stop now." I wanted to stop, but forces within held me bound. My apartment was becoming empty now because of frequent visits to the pawnshop. I just could not stop using drugs, and could not stop crying. I cried all the way to purchase dope, and cried my way back smoking it.

Then, I decided to take a bizarre ride. I intentionally drove at a speed in excess of 85 mph so that I could be pulled over by the police, only to find myself two blocks away from home. I slowed down when my strategy failed me and made a call to the Treatment Center for help. As soon as my counselor told me to drop everything and come back there, I hung up the phone. How was it possible for my mind to desire one thing while my body desired the opposite? How was it that I reached out for help, but did not desire it?

Detox Facility

December 2006 came around very quickly. In the midst of all the insanity, an idea dawned on me. I was on a four-year felony probation for leading the police on a 45-minute chase at Port Arthur, TX. My instinct told me to turn myself in to them. I searched for the phone and called my probation officer. I told her exactly what I was planning to do. She immediately hung up the phone. Thirty minutes later, there were two police officers at my door. There were many times in my life that I never wanted to go to jail; however, in my circumstance, going there was the best idea for me. I put my hands behind my back as if they were about to be cuffed. The perplexed police officers asked me what I was doing. I made them understand that I was prepared to go to jail, but was told that I could not be arrested for nothing – I had committed no crime, they said. I also tried to make them understand that I had violated my probation by drinking and taking drugs. They asked where the drugs were – they certainly saw an insane fellow here. I owned up that I had taken them all, and showed them the utensils that I used. The police officers then put a handcuff on me, and led me away – only it was not to jail. They transported me to a Detox Facility for psychiatric help. I was given some shots upon my arrival there, and prescribed psychiatric medications. These helped for a while. The facility passed out snack baskets daily. I grabbed the baskets at every given opportunity and ate whatever was in there like a hungry animal, because I had not had a decent meal in weeks. Food was so precious to me at the facility that I ended up fighting for it. After about a week, I was released from the Detox Facility.

CHAPTER 3

The Treatment Center (II)

My mind cleared up after a week of sobriety at the Detox Facility. It had been my usual habit to sell anything I could lay my hands on, to raise money for drugs. When I went back to my apartment and saw what was left of my possessions, I was determined to sell-off everything with the hope of running out of sellable items that were enabling me to replenish my drugs.

My escapist tendencies cropped up as usual to blot out the hard realities of my self-destructive lifestyle, but it suddenly dawned on me that I had to put a stop to all the craziness. I left the apartment and drove back to the Treatment Center for help. There were no beds available at the center, but I was given the option to stick around, in case one became vacant by chance. Since I had nowhere else worth going back to, I hung around. I was fortunate that a client failed to show up from work. His bed was assigned to me.

I was a hopeless thirty-one year old man when I checked into the Treatment Center to seek help a second time. I was a shadow of my former self and obviously unhealthy. My Clothing Size was 28, and I weighed just 105 lbs. One of my sisters came to the center to take away the 2005 two-door Honda Accord Coupe that was presented to me when I was of good behavior and striving to get my life back. I knew that I was never going to get my car back when she drove it away. This time around, I was very honest with my sisters, the counselors, and the psychiatrist. I narrated my three suicide attempts to the psychiatrist. I had once taken a cocktail of medications to end it all, but woke up to find myself in a hospital bed where the medications were being pumped out of my stomach. I cut my wrist a few times as well, but the cuts were not deep enough to cause enough blood loss that would bring my life to a complete halt. My last attempt at suicide was to jump off a bridge. I successfully had one hand hanging out, but was not courageous enough to let myself go. I was too afraid to finish the job. I was at my lowest ebb at the time, and exhausted by my way of living. I did not want to live to see another day of agony. I did not want to seek solace in alcohol and drugs any longer, and the only way I knew how to put a stop to it all was to commit suicide.

This was the first time that I was open and honest with anyone, and more importantly, myself. The psychiatrist told me at the conclusion of his evaluation that I had suffered various psychiatric conditions. I was then prescribed psychiatric medications. I was taking twelve pills in the morning, and nine at night. I was desperate to do whatever it took to get better at that point, so I started to pay attention in the classes that they offered at the center, and listened to individuals who brought their stories of strength and hope. I was continuously reminded that my hope for recovery was the intervention of God, and the completion of a 12-Step Process. The importance of willingly seeking God for a turnaround was emphasized. It was up to me. I later got myself a sponsor who guided me through the 12-Step Process, but only did what I felt was important enough to do. Gladly, I successfully completed the program at the center and transitioned to an Oxford House - a home for people determined to learn to live without the use of drugs and alcohol.

CHAPTER 4

Oxford House

It was April 2007. I was hired at a call center for a dental company. I had always dreamed of working there, and was thrilled about this development. Things were picking up for me once again. My parents saw the progress I was making and gave me one of their vehicles. Today, I realize that I was a very ungrateful man. I was never satisfied with anything I had. I wanted more, and better. I do not know if it was my diet, the psychiatric medication I was taking, or a combination of both, but I noticed that I had put on a lot of weight - I was a Clothing Size 36, and weighed over 170 lbs. I felt uncomfortable about my weight and decided to hit the gym. After several weeks, I decided to give drinking one more chance. I started to drink inside my room at the Oxford House. At first, I told myself that I was not going to be hooked on drugs again, but I continuously lied to myself as usual. After a few weeks of binge drinking and drug abuse, guilt and shame got hold of me. I knew the folks at the Oxford House were aware of my waywardness, so, I decided to move out of the place voluntarily before I was kicked out. I left my things at the Oxford House, and found an apartment complex nearby. The tenants in the apartment complex were either using or selling drugs. The area became a comfort zone for me as a chronic addict, myself. I parked my car there, and lived in it for the next two months.

I needed money as time went on. It was no surprise then, that my next adventure was to locate an ATM Machine nearby. I gathered over two thousand five hundred dollars from my bank account and made it to a motel. With so much money and drugs at my disposal, I soon lost my senses. My mind was running wild with delusions of being poisoned by an invisible guest that was staying with me in the motel room. I was completely out of touch with reality, and in a world of my own – drinking excessively, getting high on drugs, and watching adult movies all day long.

CHAPTER 5

The Upper Room
Father's Perfect Revelation

I had not slept in days. I had not eaten in days. I had not showered in weeks. The only thing I was doing was drinking, and getting high on drugs. I was saddened to have been a disappointment all my life, and believed that my family would be better off without me. *This world would be a better place without you, Susehg.* I often thought.

Again, I sat down watching adult movies. As I flipped the channels on the TV, a certain man grabbed my attention. He was a pastor speaking about God. I burst into tears immediately and reached for my drug utensil. As I was about to take a hit, my hands began to shake uncontrollably. I instantly threw the drug utensil into the trash, breaking it to pieces as it hit one of the beer bottles lying around. I was now breathing heavily. I knew that something or someone was with me in that room. I was sane enough to know that, but told myself that I was going to continue taking my drugs regardless of what was happening. I had an extra drug utensil in the drawer; so, I reached for it. Once the drug preparation was set for me to take, my hands began to shake again. I threw the utensil away at that point; feeling terrified, and began to yell on top of my lungs for help. For some strange reason, it dawned on me that I was going to get help somehow on this day. The television set was still on the Church channel, with the speakers talking about an Upper Room. In the midst of the confusion, I felt something moving me to the window and opening the drapes wide. I unconsciously stood in front of the window with my arms spread out, and in came the strongest gust of wind I had ever felt in my life. I could not move, as the strong wind blew right through me. The only thing that I was able to do was yell uncontrollably for help. Suddenly, I felt a soothing touch on my neck, and experienced a sensational feeling that I am unable to

> **"The wind blows where it wants, and you hear the sound thereof, but cannot tell from where it comes, and where it goes: so is every one that is born of the Spirit." (John 3:8)**

express. It was so perfect, that I immediately surrendered. Father carried me to the bed and laid me down. I had the urge to take another hit of drugs while I was lying down and tried to reach for my utensil. Then I heard a *Voice* say, *"Once you stop fighting, you will allow Me to fight for you."* I started to say some things. I recall now that what I said at the time was something I had to do in the future.

I got up and sat in front of the TV with my hands on the bed, bending as far back as possible. There were two men now talking about a Father. I turned around, looked up to the top right corner of the room, and heard a *Voice* say to me, *"You will be my son, and I will be your Father."* I turned back to the TV and noticed that it was static. Then, I placed my hands on the static TV feeling very sad to the point of breaking down in tears. I looked up to the top right corner of the room again, hoping to find the person whose voice I heard, but saw no one.

It was certain now that I was no longer in control of what I was doing - the Holy Spirit had taken over. I grabbed the keys to my car and left the room, perplexed. I started to drive the car with both hands on the steering wheel since I felt weak. I wanted to roll down the window and turn the radio on, but realized that I could not. Again, the unimaginable force restrained me. I began to yell again. The force took me right to the front door of a police building. I knocked very hard on the door, but there was no answer. I then returned to my car and started to head downtown at a very high speed. I ran through all the red lights and almost caused an accident. After a while, I stepped out of the car with my arms on top of the car, waiting to be arrested; but no cop showed up. After about five minutes of waiting, I got into the car again and drove speedily to a destination I did not know. As I approached the opposite side of a train track, I heard one of my tires blow out. I drove the car to the front of the train station and abandoned it there. As I was walking away very slowly, I said to other passersby on the road, "I do not know what I am doing. Please help me." I was running around aimlessly, and almost naked. Then I did something very strange. I got on my knees and urged a young girl to place her hands on mine. My tone was gradually becoming aggressive as I continued to plead with her. When she took off and began to run away from me, I got up and chased after her. Within a few minutes, I had unconsciously caused a scene and drawn a crowd.

A young man stopped my wild-goose chase and asked what was going on, but I could not explain myself. I knelt in front of him and pledged to offer him some money, if he could help get the girl that was running from me and make her place her hands on mine. "How much money do you have?" he asked. I had hundreds of dollars on me at the time, so I reached into my cargo shorts pocket and showed him what I had. He immediately snatched the money and ran away with it. As he snatched the money from me, some of the bills fell to the ground. Everyone around helped themselves to what appeared to be free money. I later found myself standing motionless in front of another man, with my arms straight down on both sides. The man hit me right in the jaw. I heard the sirens of an ambulance and a police vehicle as I slowly fell backwards to the ground. I knew they were coming for me, even though I no longer had my senses at that point. The ambulance transported me to the psychiatric ward of a hospital, where I was held down and given several shots in the buttocks. I lay helpless and unconscious in the psychiatric ward, for three days.

CHAPTER 6

A Drink to Remember

I awoke in my hospital bed very confused, but managed to call one of my sisters to pick me up. She drove me to Plano, TX. My other sister allowed me to recuperate at her apartment. Mind you, I had been missing in action for over a month before I contacted my sisters. I had been living in my car and spending time under a bridge, drinking and getting high on drugs.

It had been almost two months since I enjoyed a good rest. I was offered a bed, where I slept like a log. I went over to the kitchen when I woke up, slapped two slices of bread together with some ham, and ate hungrily. I noticed two bottles on the table as I was eating - one had very little vodka in it, and the other, wine. There was not a single thought in me to stay away from the bottles. As I mentioned before, the sight of alcohol alone often stirred up instant reaction in me. I grabbed the bottle of vodka and gulped down what was left in it. What I was feeling at that point was not strange at all. *I am about to get drunk, anyway.* I thought to myself. I searched desperately for a cork to open the second bottle, took a sip of wine, and put it down for a moment. The sensation of alcohol was now setting in as I took some wine. I intended to drink the whole bottle to satisfy my insatiable desire for this weird sensation - only this time, my plan did not go far. As I held the bottle of wine in my hand to continue drinking, my bottom jaw suddenly shifted to the left. My tongue had also curled back to the end of my throat. It was as though something in my gut was pulling and holding on to it. I slowly put the bottle of wine down, hoping my bewildering experience was a temporary one. The longer I stood there, the more it dawned on me that my bottom jaw was locked on one side. I was breathing heavily now and unable to talk.

Suddenly, the entire right side of my body was numb. I stood frightened and confused, wondering what to do about my condition. I began to hop about. I moved to the living room, grabbed a set of keys from the table, and hopped out of the apartment to the streets. I got on a golf cart that I found there with the hope that it would transport me out of the area, but realized that I did not have the keys to move it. I continued to hop about on the street, hoping to find someone who would notice my condition and reach out to me. I needed help so badly on this fateful day, but not a single vehicle was coming or going either way on the 15th street in Plano, Texas. It suddenly dawned on me that it was Sunday – everyone was at church. The thought of that dashed my hope of getting immediate help.

I eventually made it across the street and hopped into the tobacco store that was open. I continued to hope that I would get help, and someone would at least call 911 immediately. Several people ran to me and asked if everything was fine. I made some indistinct sounds since I could no longer speak, and motioned with my left hand to write. One of the men around understood my gesture and ran to get me a pen and paper, with which I wrote, "Call 911." I was breathing so heavily with the little writing effort I made, so I hopped outside to get some air. Not too long after, I heard the siren of an ambulance that was approaching the store. I groaned loudly in pain as two men strapped me onto a stretcher and carted me off the ground to the waiting ambulance. The pain in my body had escalated significantly by the time I was placed in the ambulance. The pain was so severe, that I felt like my entire body was about to break into two – I felt like a mere pencil that you could easily break into two halves. The paramedics tried to calm me down as I was groaning loudly for help, but the excruciating pain was more than I could bear. I passed out after a few minutes.

The Intensive Care Unit

I awoke to find myself in the ICU unit of a hospital. I could barely move. There were tubes running all over my body. I was shocked to find that a urinary catheter had been placed in me as well. When I regained consciousness, I asked the nurse what happened to me, and was informed that I suffered a terrible stroke due to a combination of alcohol and psychiatric medications intake. When she said, "combination," I immediately remembered the shots I was given at the psychiatric ward prior to taking alcohol at my sister's place. The nurse asked if I needed anything. I had never felt so hungry in my entire existence, so I asked for food. I ate hungrily like a man that had not eaten in years.

My sisters later came up to visit me. Have you ever had anyone love you so much, only to find that you are consistently in a pathetic situation? What had my sisters not done for me? What had they not given me? What had they not said to encourage and support me? My family had grown accustomed to my way of life over the years, even though they never knew how things got so bad. They never once questioned my flaws, nor said things to embarrass me - all out of love. Whenever they heard from me (months after my disappearance), I was either in jail, or caught up in potentially embarrassing situations. Their love for me never ceased, but their patience was now running thin. Once, I saw my mother's expression change within a split second. The son she had not heard from in weeks suddenly appeared at the front door looking frail and unkempt. He had neither eaten a decent meal nor showered in weeks. She had gone from a happy mother of a bubbling son, to a disheartened one, seeing him destroy his life. I disappointed my family so much, and just could not do anything to make things right.

I was later transferred to a single 24-hour suicide watch room. I recovered from my stroke soon after, and was able to move around fully again. Towards the end of my two-week stay at the hospital, a nurse came into my room and asked me a few simple questions: "Sir, your time is coming to an end. Whom do you want to call? Where do you want to go?" My mind was completely blank now. I had run out of possible solutions. I turned my head to the side and cried my heart out like a baby. I was tired of putting myself through this, year after year. I hated myself for not being able to do anything right, and wondered why I did the things that I did. *Who in this world would look*

> **The LORD is near to them that are of a broken heart; and saves such as be of a contrite spirit. (Psalm 34:18)**

and see something in me that was worth looking at? I kept wondering.

That evening a very tall man came into my room, but said nothing to me. He just handed me a card. On it was the name of the same Detox Facility that the police officers transported me to when I had an episode. I held up the card to the nurse and asked to be transferred there. After spending a week at the Detox Facility, I was again transferred to another facility. The facility was an all-too-familiar place – the Treatment Center. I stepped out of a van and stood in front of the Treatment Center that I had visited twice already in the past two years – that would be my third time there in those two years. My body was exhausted, but my mind was not. Have you ever stood in front of a place with no one around, but felt that you were being tugged left and right? That was how I felt. *Not again!* I thought to myself. I wanted to run as far as I possibly could, away from this place. I did not hate the Treatment Center, but I concluded that seeking help there was going to be a complete waste of time. I lost hope in finding help from every other angle as well. I had lived an extremely reckless lifestyle for over a decade. My family reached out to me so many times and did all in their power to help me succeed, but I failed them, time after time.

CHAPTER 7

The Treatment Center (III)

In less than two years in Dallas, Texas, I had been at this Treatment Center three times. I had also been at the Detox Facility twice, received treatment at a Psychiatric Ward, and spent time at an Intensive Care Unit.

They welcomed me at the Treatment Center with open arms, just as they had always done. I was very quiet this time around, and accepted the fact that I knew nothing about myself. There was also a significant change in treatment - I was assigned a different counselor. Instead of a man, I had a young female counselor. She was an intelligent, attractive, and sophisticated woman, with no history of alcohol or drug addiction. Change was something I never liked. I felt uncomfortable about having this woman as my counselor at first. I wanted someone who had been out there, just like I had: someone that I could relate to; someone who had walked in my shoes and felt my pain. I was later to find out that she would be more help to me than I envisaged.

It was crucial for me to discuss my *Upper Room* experience at the motel room with my counselor. I told her exactly what happened. "Were you aware of what you were doing?" she asked. "No," I simply answered. She then counseled me on the next step to take. She told me it was important to go through the 12-Step Process. I had attempted the 12-Step Process twice before, but was not honest with the staff working with me. The truth was that, I did not feel compelled to share the key events in my past with anyone at the time. These were events that I did not feel comfortable bringing up. I tried so hard to forget them, but the harder I tried to pretend that they did not occur, the more I remembered them too well.

"There is a step in the 12-Step Process that requires you to go back to the individual, open up about what you did, and make amends," my counselor said. "You've got to be kidding me!" I said to myself. It was hard enough for me to admit what I did. Now I had to tell someone about it, go back to the victims to own up to my fault, and then apologize. When the session with my counselor ended, I began to see things the way I never saw them before. I looked all around the meeting room and saw myself in each of the other clients there. I realized that I never knew what the word *prejudice* meant. I always thought it merely had to do with racism. How wrong I was! I realized there and then that I hated who I was so much, that I hated anyone who drank heavily and took drugs like I did. I had no compassion for them, and never gave myself a chance to make things right, either.

Suffice it to say I kept to myself throughout my time at the Treatment Center. I got my act together this time around, and made it a point to attend every meeting that was offered – even on Saturdays. You were only required to attend one of their two meetings, but I attended both – that was how determined I was. I sought the help of a man who had been coming to the facility regularly for the previous three Saturday nights that I was there, to guide me through the 12-Step Process.

Discovering Myself

As I was going through the 12-Step Process, I began to discover myself – who I really was, and why I hated myself. At some point in my troubled times, I had lost the power to love and care for myself. I told my ex-wife so many times that I loved her, but I never did. Not once did I express the love I thought I had for her. I did not know what it meant to love anyone. I never loved myself; it was little wonder then that I was incapable of loving anyone. I could not give what I did not have.

Soon after discovering my true self, I noticed that I began to do things differently. I put myself in others' shoes and cultivated compassion. I watched myself through others. This enabled me to begin to make good judgments and wise decisions. The best gift anyone can have is the ability to speak; but I learnt to be quiet, speaking only when it was necessary.

As my time at the Treatment Center was about to end, I gave up on my own ideas of doing things. I began to practice giving my entire life to God. I relied solely on Him. I am glad to say that has been the case to date. I learnt that it was important to practice a thing day in, and day out, if one wanted to be perfect at it. It has turned out to be so.

> **"If any man will come after Me, let him deny himself, and take up his cross daily, and follow Me." (Luke 9:23)**

The man (who then became my sponsor) that was guiding me through the 12-Step Process told me about a place not too far from the Treatment Center, that would give me the opportunity to live on their premises and continue to work towards achieving sustained recovery. It was the Home of Sobriety.

CHAPTER 8

The Home of Sobriety

My sponsor drove me to the Home of Sobriety - a halfway house for alcoholics and drug addicts. It was a glorified jail, so to speak. I stepped out of the car with trash bags containing the few things I had to my name. The place charged seven dollars a day to sleep on a mat in a meeting room. The room was truly set up for client meetings, but I guess they felt the need to make money out of it for reasons I could not understand. I was assigned a school-like locker to keep my belongings, and strongly advised to get a lock for it. No one had to tell me what that meant. I put my belongings up and headed to the office to meet with one of the program directors, who informed me that the program they had ran for six months. I was compelled to tell him that I planned to move out of the dump when I received my pay in three weeks. I was rehired at a call center for the dental company at the time and was indeed expecting a paycheck. I wandered around the premises for a few minutes, feeling downcast. There were two other floors at the place, but it cost several more dollars a day to sleep on a bed there. Besides, there were no beds available, and I did not intend to stay longer than three weeks in a smelly halfway house, anyway.

I made it to the meeting room later in the evening, and sat with other clients to tell the story of my life. I cried as I narrated how a small-sized drug utensil almost destroyed me. They all listened to my story with rapt attention. The next client to speak must have been in his early fifties. He spoke about losing his businesses, the women he married, and his homes. He could not see his children, he said; and life for him was not worth living. *This man's situation is not as severe as mine is*, [I was thinking]. I guess I thought so, because he was just an alcoholic. I was wrong. By the time life treated him so badly, he had lost three times what I lost. He held up his right hand, and made his thumb and index finger into a letter 'C' to tell us how constant intake of shots of wine brought about his destruction. The tears in my eyes stopped rolling down my face after I listened to his story. Here was a man who was much older than I was, and had lost much more than I thought I did. I felt a glimpse of hope and began to think more clearly.

After our 8:00pm meeting that day, it was time to make our *beds* for the night. We were directed to fold up the tables and chairs, set them aside, and pull out the mats they had given us to sleep on. Sleeping on a mat meant that you had to share the restroom with everyone else. I remember waking up very early the next morning and waiting at the restroom door to take my turn. I started to hate the Home of Sobriety after staying there for a while, and just could not wait to get my paycheck so I could pay what I owed and get out of there. I stayed on at the Home of Sobriety for the next three weeks, sleeping on the miserable mat provided. I finally got my paycheck and went into the office with my belongings to pay what I owed. I really do not recall what happened during my conversation with them at the office, but I found myself moving upstairs into a bed at the place I called *Home* for the next fifty-three weeks.

CHAPTER 9

The Voice

At the Home of Sobriety, I continued the routine that I got accustomed to while at the Treatment Center. I spoke only when necessary, and focused on my recovery. I wanted to learn not just about achieving sobriety, but also maintaining it. I became more aware of myself and made efforts to change for the better, daily.

One afternoon, my mind took the image of a female news reporter on TV. I soon realized that I was entertaining immoral thoughts about her. The thoughts became intense as the days went by – they became quite overwhelming each time I saw a woman on TV. My mind was playing games on me, but the Lord had me safely wrapped up in His loving arms. I continued to have these weird fantasies until my instincts suddenly told me one day to stop watching TV, and get up. I immediately went back to the room on this day, and lay on my bunk. Then I heard a *Voice* instructing me not to watch TV until I was ready. From

**Therefore, if any man be in Christ, he is a new creature: old things are passed away; behold, all things are become new.
(2 Corinthians 5:17)**

that moment on, I watched TV only on Sundays. I watched nothing but football until the summer of the following year. I wanted so badly to change, and was determined to do whatever was necessary to have a NEW ME.

> *"You will look the way I want you to look. You will walk the way I want you to walk. You will see what I want you to see. You will sound the way I want you to sound. You will know only what I allow you to know. You will be who I want you to be."*

These, were the words I heard. The *Voice* guided me in becoming who I am today. *It* also instructed me to volunteer my time. Never in my previous life did I get myself involved in anything that did not benefit me. It was always about me – just me.

I found a place Downtown Dallas where I could volunteer my time, and registered there. I gave two hours of my time each day after work, for the next six weeks, knowing fully well that I would not be compensated financially. I also made it a point to volunteer my time at the Treatment Center (the place I had been before the Home of Sobriety) at weekends, in spite of my busy weekday schedule. I wanted to go there because I believed that the assistance they gave me was instrumental to my recovery. I felt obliged to give back, and was delighted to help in the kitchen.

The Gift of Giving

As I was trying to sleep one night, the *Voice* instructed me to do something that I thought was ridiculous. It told me to withdraw a certain amount of money from my bank account. The money was not mine to keep – it was to be given away. I had never heard of such a thing. Giving money away was something that I had never thought of doing before. I lay

> **Give, and it shall be given unto you; good measure, pressed down, and shaken together, and running over, shall men give into your lap. For with the same measure that you measure it shall be measured to you again. (Luke 6:38)**

there for another hour or so, but the *Voice* kept repeating the instruction. I finally gave up, but grumbled while I was putting on some clothes. I went to an ATM machine to withdraw the money, and sat on the bench on the front porch, patiently waiting for the recipient of the money. I was soon to receive a sign. A fellow client at the Home of Sobriety suddenly appeared. He sat right next to me and began to tell me of his financial troubles. He could not come up with his rent, he said, and was about to be evicted from the place unless he came up with at least half of what he owed. I gave him the money I withdrew from the ATM without questions, and told him not to tell anyone about it. I continued with this charitable deed for the remainder of my stay at the Home of Sobriety, and took it as a sign that I was not to hesitate to help anyone who ever talked to me about having problems paying their rent. I had a very addictive personality, and instead of being addicted to drugs and alcohol, my Father had me addicted to *Giving*. Today, I give generously without giving any thought for my own benefit. I had been instructed by the *Voice* to give my best asset if there was nothing to give – that best asset would be, *Myself*.

Giving

Being in a position to give is a Blessing itself. Give in secret, so that only the Lord will know. Do not boast or make your Giving known. You are not giving because of Him when you give and make it known. Do everything in secret, for all secrets are known to Him; and you shall be rewarded openly for what you have done in secret, in His Name.

(Matthew 6:2-4)

Bless your body, Bless your soul, and Bless your spirit, as the Father thanks you for doing things in secret, in Him, and for Him.

Bible Lessons with Father

Towards the end of 2007, I was given a book that I thought I would never read. I could never comprehend anything that I read in my years of schooling. I frankly do not recall ever reading a book in its entirety. I cheated in every class, and thought going to school was a waste of time.

I had seen this book once before in my early twenties, and now owned one. There were no pictures in the book, and the title contained just two words – words so small and compact. Yet, I thought it would take a lifetime to finish reading it. I never saw this coming, but I was going to read the Holy Bible word for word, with my Father. I had a four-hour commute to, and from work, and read the Bible on the bus for five months. I started to get a deeper knowledge of my Father as I was reading it. Some of the words were very hard to pronounce and I did not know what they meant. I would skip the words that I could not pronounce and pretend that the words that I did not understand were not important to me. That did not last long, as the Holy Spirit soon arrested me. He gave me the proper pronunciation for the words that I could not pronounce, and I got two dictionaries to look up the words that had no meaning to me. My Father knew how impatient I was, and how I read every word as if it was just one syllable. As I was reading the Bible one day, the *Voice* said to me, *"Slow Down! You will not only read every word in this Book; you will also pronounce every letter of each word. You will not rush this Bible as you have rushed everything in your life."* The words came with much power and authority.

CHAPTER 10

Great Miracles

The Cross

I have noted almost everything that happened to me since that evening in the motel room, when I had the *Upper Room* experience. I realize several things about myself now that I never paid close attention to. The fourth finger of my right hand has two lines that intersect each other in the form of a cross. I do not know if this was on me all my life, or appeared just recently; but I can recall vividly where I was when I saw it for the very first time. I was on a bus. If you look at your palm, you will notice that there are lines running back and forth. I have those lines too, with two extra ones in the form of the Holy Cross. The cross is not tattooed - I have never had a tattoo before, nor thought of getting one. I was hysterical when I first noticed the cross and did not understand why such a magnificent symbol was implanted on my finger.

My Circumcision

I had heard of circumcision; but I was not circumcised, since I was born in a hut in Vietnam. I thought of ways to get circumcised when I began to gain deeper knowledge of my Father. I did not know how much the

> **"This is My covenant, which you shall keep, between Me and you and your seed after you; Every man child among you shall be circumcised."**
> **(Genesis 17:10)**

procedure would cost, but planned to call around to find out.

One morning while I was changing into my work clothes in the restroom at work, I looked down at my manhood and saw something that made me fall right on my knees to praise the Almighty God. I never made one phone call to find out the cost of circumcision. My Father granted me one at no cost.

I revealed these amazing discoveries to several people, who concluded that I was delusional. They told me that I would never be fully sane because of my many years of alcohol and drug addiction. God could not manifest Himself in the life of a

> **And Jesus came and spoke to them saying, "All power is given to Me in Heaven and on earth." (Matthew 28:18)**

wretch like me, they said. They viewed all that was happening to me as one big coincidence, and recommended that I start taking my psychiatric medications again. At first, I doubted myself and began to see things their way; but I knew my healing was complete. *Perhaps, I was circumcised at birth then, and did not realize it*, I thought. Then a conversation with my mother proved otherwise. I asked her if I was circumcised at birth. She said to me, "I never knew or heard of such a thing at that time." My confidence in my Father then remained unshaken.

I have read the Bible in its entirety. I have looked up the meaning of so many words to acquire knowledge. I have had lessons with my Father. Not once, while reading the Bible, did I come across the word *coincidence*. Nothing is a coincidence with my Father. I know so. He makes all things beautiful in His own time, and arranges them for His own purposes.

CHAPTER 11

Kingdom Assignment

It was almost the end of 2007. I had been able to obtain slots at three facilities that gave me the opportunity to come in and give my testimony. The counselors at my previous Treatment Center who rotated working on Saturdays saw me there at weekends, and asked if I wanted to share my story with their 10am class. At the Home of Sobriety, where I was residing, they needed someone to chair and speak at their Wednesday night meetings at 8:00pm. There was a hospital in North Dallas that provided services to children aged twelve to seventeen who were addicted to drugs and alcohol. The hospital gave me the opportunity to testify there as well.

I felt blessed, and was extremely grateful that my Father saw me fit enough to do great things for Him. I remember having just a crowd of six to eight people the very first time I spoke at a meeting. That was enough to make me nervous. I took speech classes in college, but did not know why I took those classes at the time. Standing in front of people was something I never saw myself doing.

> "All things are delivered unto Me of My Father: and no man knows the Son, but the Father; neither knows any man the Father, except the Son, and he to whomever the Son will reveal Him." (Matthew 11:27)

All along, I was only comfortable being part of the crowd - sitting in a group and listening to a speaker. Have you ever felt like there was something that you had never done, never intended to do, but had to do it, anyway? That was how I felt. I was awfully concerned about people's impression of me. Throughout my previous life, I based my decisions on what others would think or say about me. Again, it always had to be about me. I was one of those individuals who would try very hard to meet your needs, and then pull away to leave you on your own.

It was not easy for me at first to stand in front of a crowd to give a presentation. All kinds of questions would go through my mind as I was speaking: *"Am I doing this right?" "Am I saying the right things?" "Am I helping anyone?"* I doubted and judged myself, but the Lord was there with me. After saying a short prayer at the beginning of each session, I found myself giving my testimony effortlessly. I continued to give my testimony with the help of the Lord for the next two years.

CHAPTER 12

My Trial
Father by My Side

It was February 8, 2008. A typical Friday evening it was - the traffic was at a standstill. I looked ahead of me and saw a vehicle unlawfully cutting into the Higher Occupancy Vehicle (HOV) Lane. I was not going to be late getting anywhere, neither was my house about to be burnt down, but I decided to follow suit. As I got in the HOV Lane, a white SUV hit the trunk of my car. My car miraculously slid across four lanes without hitting any other vehicle. I was tremendously shocked. As I remained in my car on the other side of the highway, still shocked and confused, the men in the white SUV began to walk towards me. I noticed that one of them was being restrained from getting close – he was obviously coming to charge at me to do more damage. After the whole episode, a friend drove down to pick me up.

I was living Downtown Dallas, and working at North Plano at the time. It was almost a two-hour drive to, and from work every day. The meeting at the hospital was also an hour away from home. I would be lying if I said that I did not have thoughts of giving up when the automobile accident occurred. This was a very good excuse for me to start drinking again.

> "You are My witnesses," says the LORD, "and My servant whom I have chosen: that you may know and believe Me, and understand that I am He: before Me there was no God formed, neither shall there be after Me."
> (Isaiah 43:10)

The day after the accident, I started to walk to the Treatment Center since I had no car. The *Voice* continually spoke to me during the walk. I looked around me and asked aloud, "Where are You?" I got on my knees in broad daylight and cried my heart out after He answered, *"Inside of you."*

I began to commute with buses and trains on a daily basis. I had taken public transportation before in the first few months of my stay in Dallas, so this was not a new thing. I would wake up at 4:45am to catch the first bus out. It was a stressful and long commute of two buses, one train, and a ten-minute walk to get to work. It took two hours to get to work, and about two and a half hours to get back home. This was my schedule, Monday through Friday, for five months. I knew my meetings were as important as my job. I would walk to the Treatment Center on Saturdays around 9:00am to deliver my speech, and then catch a bus at noon to the hospital, arriving at my destination around 3:00pm to deliver the next speech. Sunday was my day of rest. I kept to this schedule as well, for five months.

CHAPTER 13

Life after the Home of Sobriety
Year 2008

It had been a year since my stay at the Home of Sobriety. As much as I was very thankful to be there, I knew my time was about to end. Alcohol and drugs had not found their way into my body the whole year. I was completely sober.

It was *Presentation Day* at the Home of Sobriety. This was a very special day planned to celebrate those who successfully completed their program. I recall that I was very proud of myself on the night that I was to be presented for this laudable achievement. The last time I remember being sober before then, was 1993 - I was sixteen. I have to admit that the Year 2008 was one of the best years of my life. I had a purpose in life with achievable goals that were unfolding. Most importantly, I had my Heavenly Father, who remolded and gave me a second chance to fulfill His original purpose for my life. When my name was called, I immediately fell on my knees, held out my hands, and praised the Lord Almighty God in the presence of everyone. There was silence in the room in that brief moment. People knew then that I belonged to Him.

All my things were packed! I was ready to launch out. I never thought a day would come that I would be in a position to rent an apartment. Having been on probation, I knew it was going to take a miracle to be approved for an apartment. My poor credit history was not encouraging, either. Today, I know better – My Father is a Miracle-Worker. With Him, nothing is impossible (Matthew 19:26). I moved out of the Home of Sobriety on July 3, 2008. Before I left, I fell on my knees in front of the place to give thanks to the Lord. I remember how deliriously happy I was to be moving into my first apartment. It was unbelievable that I was able to keep a job for more than a year, put aside money to pay for an apartment, and fend for myself without assistance from anyone.

I had been working for the dental company at the call center in Plano, TX for over a year and was interested in working at one of their other offices. Gladly, I secured a position there. The office was less than a mile away from my apartment. I was now waking up at 7am to catch the first bus out instead of 4:45am. What's more, it only took ten minutes on the bus to get to work. Everything seemed as perfect as it could be at this time in my life, except for one snag - I felt disgusted at the way the dentist was swindling patients of their money. My feelings culminated in an argument with the dentist once, in the manager's office. The dentist wanted me fired because of that one incident, but I was transferred to a different office instead. My transfer meant that the perfect commute that I enjoyed was over. I was not expecting it at the time, but had to accept my fate. I assumed duties at this new office, where I met her.

Undeniable Feelings

I met her on October 22, 2008. She was married. I developed very strong feelings for her in spite of her status. I must confess that I had never had such feelings for a woman before in my life. I found myself feeling guilty at the bus stop after work, and asking my Father to forgive me for harboring romantic feelings for her. I consistently prayed to have these feelings blotted out of my mind, only to wake up and fall right back in love with her, each time we saw. In the morning, I was in love with her; in the evening, I was asking for the Lord's forgiveness. I was glad that I did not have to see her on weekends, but could not wait to see her again on Monday morning. This was not something that I was proud of, but I guess I gave in to my feelings and erred as a human being. I eventually made my feelings known to her and apologized.

Twenty Twelve

It was the summer of 2009. I bought my very first car. The car was sold to me for less than one thousand dollars, but it did not matter to me that it was cheaper than the other cars I had driven. I was filled with pride and joy that I was now able to support myself. Not only was I able to solely pay my rent and bills, but I was also capable of purchasing a car with my own earned income. *Things could not be better at my current state* [or so, I thought]. Unfortunately, I was about to lose everything again, to find myself at Twenty Twelve.

On July 24, 2009, the Office Manager at the Dental Center discovered that I had been changing figures on bills for procedures, to benefit patients. She reprimanded for my action, informing me that I risked losing my job if it happened again. I was eventually sent home the following Monday. I stayed at home that week. I did a *no-call/no-show*, so to speak. Realizing later that I needed my job, I called the Office Manager the following week to ask if I could come back. She turned down my request and filed my situation as a case of Job Abandonment.

Suffice it to say that I was on a downward spiral after losing my job. Things were not looking good at all. On September 28, 2009, I vacated my apartment and moved into my sister's house at McKinney, TX. I began to read the Bible every single day since I had so much time on my hands. I packed up my belongings after much pondering and moved to Twenty Twelve on the 2nd day of October. It was at Twenty Twelve that I started to write *Servant of the LORD, Book One*. Unknowingly, I would keep it for five years before placing it in the hands of the person who would edit, and guide me into publishing it.

CHAPTER 14

My Consecration

A New Garment

"Do not ever interfere with what I am doing for you. Timing is key in life! Practice knowing time and life belong to Me."

Father impressed so many words of caution upon my heart – these were some of them. I had to remind myself always, that my life was no longer mine, and that there was never a time it was mine. It had always belonged to my Father. I had to keep learning not to interfere

> **"For I know that my redeemer lives, and that He shall stand at the latter day upon the earth: And though after my skin is thus destroyed, yet in my flesh shall I see God."**
> **(Job 19:25-26)**

with what He did for me, and through me. When I surrendered my life to Jesus Christ, I became His son. I am also a joint heir with Him to a glorious inheritance, and a chosen one of royal priesthood. He has reserved a place for me in Heaven, where I shall reign with Him according to Revelation 20:4-6. For these, I feel so blessed and privileged.

I was of use to no one - not even myself, but my Father saw me, loved me, remolded me, and made me the person I am today. I truly believe that I would not be alive to testify of His existence with my story, if He had not visited me at that motel room. Drugs and alcohol would have snuffed out my life. I was reborn in that room and given a new soul by the indwelling of the Holy Spirit, who now has absolute control of my life.

Today, I am a completely new creature. I dare not utter swear words, whereas my tongue was foul in the past. I now walk the streets with confidence, knowing my identity in Christ. I have compassion and sympathy for every human being I come across. I am much more intelligent than I ever imagined. I am now a priceless soul because of my Father. I look up to the sky sometimes and ask Him, "Why me, Father?" Then I realize that He owes no one any explanation. He simply does as He pleases. His thoughts are not our thoughts; neither are our ways His ways (Isaiah 55:8). Who am I then to question Him?

I want a closer relationship with my Father. They say, "Practice Makes Perfect." I want to put my love for Him into practice. I am not satisfied knowing my Father from the Bible. I want Him to continue to manifest Himself in me. I want Him to breathe through me. I have dedicated myself completely to my Father, and desire that He uses me as He pleases, for His glory.

A New Name

The *Voice* of the Father said to me, *"Onto you I will give a name like no other. You will take this name as I have taken you."* The name, **Susehg Tsirch**, was given to me by my Heavenly Father. I was given this new name because of my commitments to Him and the changes that occurred in my life. My first name **Susehg** is two syllables, and pronounced as **Su sehg (Sej)**. The **T** in my last name is silent, and the name is pronounced as **Search**.

"If any man serves Me, let him follow Me; and where I am, there shall also My servant be: if any man serves Me, him will My Father honor." (John 12:26)

For over three months after I was given this name, I told myself that I could not possibly accept, and answer to it. To me, it was unheard of that anyone at my age would have his entire name changed.

However, the *Voice* kept talking to me about the matter.

My former name is **Tai Dai Nguyen**. I was born in a hut in Vietnam, in 1976. I migrated to America in 1979 with my parents. At the time, my mom made a mistake on my year of birth. Instead of having it as 1976, I was born in 1975 on paper. The accurate day, month, and year of my birth no longer interest me.

We all are one lifetime away from standing to face the judgment of God. We have goals that we want to achieve in life. We also have desires. We want to lead successful lifestyles and remain relevant. As children, we were asked what we wanted to be when we grew up. We had childish dreams and gave our most creative answers as innocent little ones. Today, we live in human reality as adults, and have become who we are.

I know that I dreamt of having a woman that I cannot continue to speak about. I also wanted to be somebody that I never became. Now, I have goals that are set only by my Father. My achievements today and tomorrow all belong to Him. I want to serve Him as long as possible - until I breathe my last here, on earth. I want to make it to Heaven. I want to serve my Father until eternity. Once, I asked Him on my knees if I could be His Servant forever. He replied, *"How dare you ask such a thing?"* *"GRANTED!"*

www.ingramcontent.com/pod-product-compliance
Lightning Source LLC
Chambersburg PA
CBHW070306100426
42743CB00011B/2366